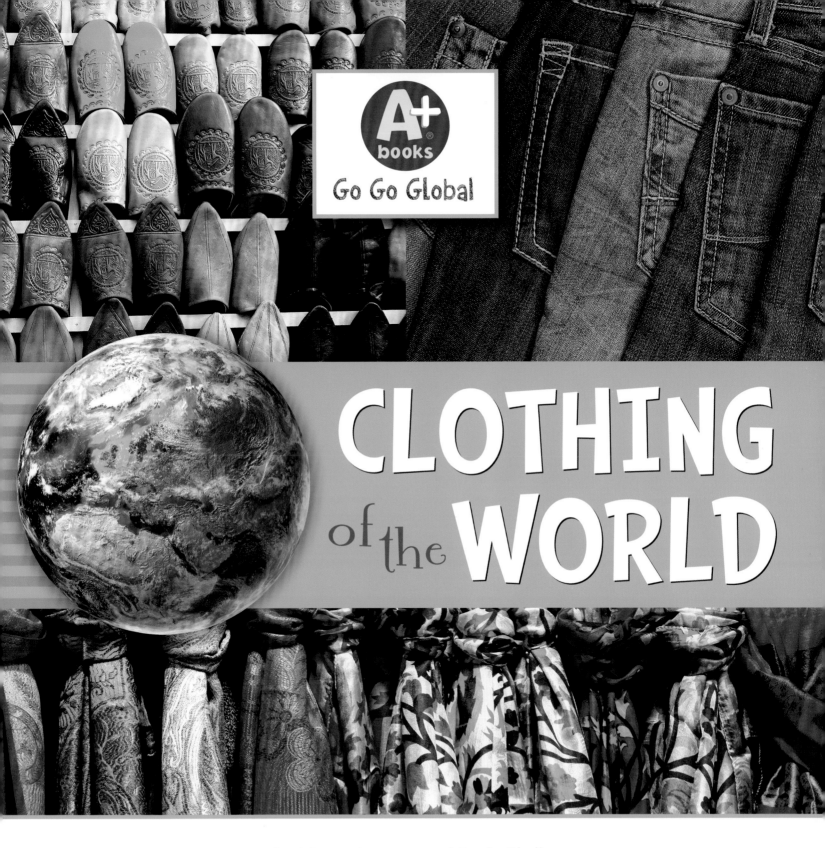

CLOTHING of the WORLD

by Nancy Loewen and Paula Skelley

CAPSTONE PRESS
a capstone imprint

Hats, coats, pants, and skirts ...

Peru

shoes, shorts,

Cuba

Pakistan

South Africa

Indonesia

shawls, and
shirts—

3

from the **tops** of our **heads**

Russia

Poland

to the **tips** of our **toes,**

4

around the **world**

India

we all wear **clothes.**

Hats for **work**,

United States

Benin

hats for **play**,

Scotland

6

Mongolia

hats for celebrations ...

Ukraine

hats for **warmth,**

Vietnam

hats for **shade,**

8

Norway

Colombia

India

hats for **special** occasions.

9

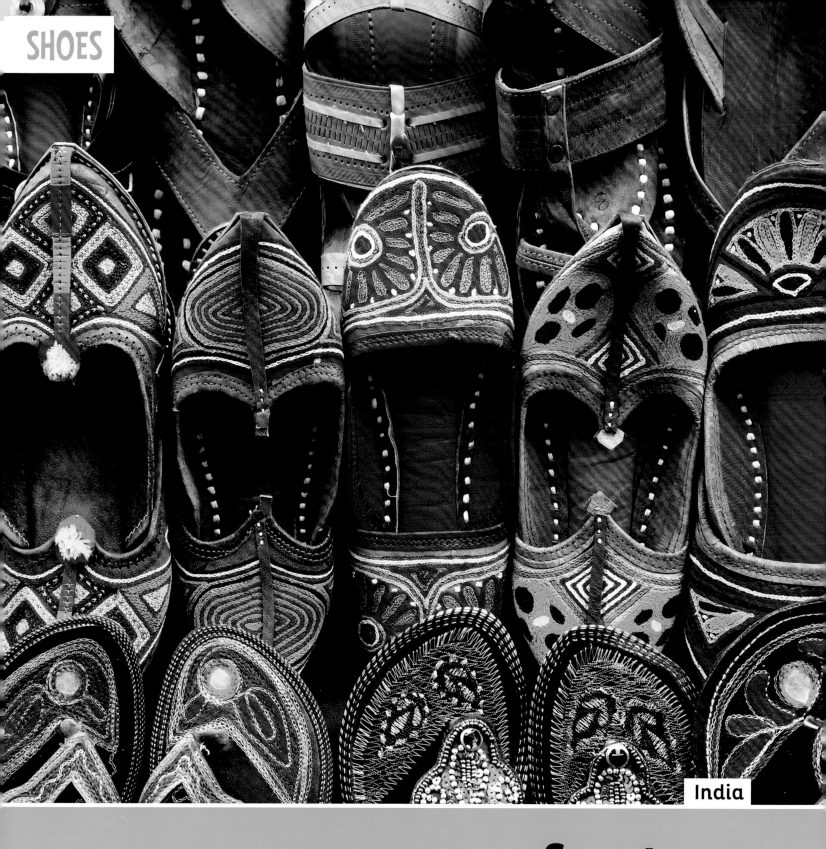

India

Now let's see what's on our feet,

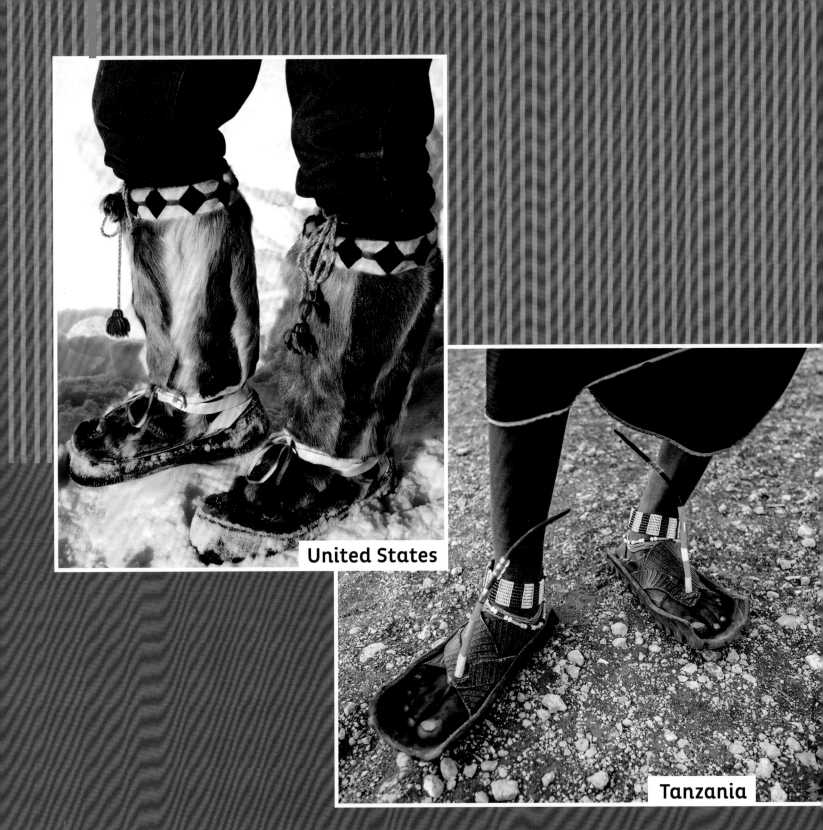

United States

Tanzania

protecting us from **cold** and **heat.**

Ethiopia

Slide

them **on**.

Tie the
laces.

United States

Ready,
shoes?

New Zealand

Let's **go places!**

Off to school!

Mexico

Germany

India

What will **YOU** wear?

China

A **shirt** with a **collar** or a **dress** with a **flare?**

Will you **put on** a **sweater?**

Ireland

How about a **tie?**

Vietnam

Whatever you wear,

United States

wear school clothes with pride.

Time to play!

Ethiopia

Let's have some fun–

China

18

in the
rain

Ukraine

or
in the
sun.

Canada 19

England

Play in **water** ...

Australia

Bulgaria

play in **snow** ...

Burundi

run so
fast ...

go, go, **go!**

Tanzania

Argentina

Some **clothes** have a **special** mission:

Czech Republic

24

Russia

to **honor** the **past** and
show **tradition**.

United States

China

Japan

silks and
bows ...

clothes

here and **now** ...

China

Spain

from long **ago**.

NORTH
AMERICA

United
States

Mexico

Cuba

Colombia

Peru

SOUTH
AMERICA

Argentina

Norway

Scotland

Ireland

England

Germany

EUROPE

Poland

Ukraine

Bulgaria

Spain

Czech Republic

Pakistan

AFRICA

Ethiopia

Benin

Burundi

Tanzania

South
Africa

ANTARCTICA

Russia

ASIA

Mongolia

China

Japan

India

Vietnam

Indonesia

AUSTRALIA

Australia

New Zealand

GLOSSARY

celebration—activities that mark a special day

collar—a band or strap worn around the neck

flare—a spreading outward at the bottom

honor—to give praise or show respect

mission—a planned job or task

occasion—a special or important event

pride—a feeling that one has worth and importance

protect—to keep safe

shawl—a piece of soft material that is worn over the shoulders or around the head

tradition—a custom, idea, or belief passed down through time

CRITICAL THINKING USING THE COMMON CORE

1. Name three reasons why a person might wear a hat. (Key Ideas and Details)

2. Which clothes in this book are most like yours? Which clothes are most unlike yours? How are they different? (Integration of Knowledge and Ideas)

3. Look at the clothes in the Cultural section. Explain how they are different from play clothes or school clothes. (Integration of Knowledge and Ideas)

A+ Books are published by Capstone Press,
1710 Roe Crest Drive, North Mankato, Minnesota 56003
www.capstonepub.com

Library of Congress Cataloging-in-Publication Data
Cataloging-in-publication information is on file with the Library
of Congress.
ISBN 978-1-4914-3917-3 (library binding)
ISBN 978-1-4914-3928-9 (paperback)
ISBN 978-1-4914-3938-8 (eBook PDF)

Editorial Credits
Jill Kalz, editor; Juliette Peters, designer; Tracy Cummins,
media researcher; Tori Abraham, production specialist

Photo Credits
Alamy: Michele and Tom Grimm, 11 Left; Shutterstock: Alena Ozerova,
19 Top, Alexandra Lande, 14 Bottom, Andrea Obzerova, 4 Bottom,
Andresr, 17, Andy Dean Photography, 14 TL, Anton_Ivanov, 6 BL, 12 Top,
18 Top, aphotostory, 27 Top, aslysun, 18 Bottom, bikeriderlondon, Cover
BR, Dasha Petrenko, 13, De Visu, 4 Top, Digital Media Pro, 26, Distinctive
Images, 3 BR, Filip Fuxa, Cover TL, Goran Bogicevic, 2, ISchmidt, 19
Bottom, Jeanne Provost, 6 Top, Kanokratnok, 11 Right, 24 TL, katatonia82,
1 Bottom, kolo5, 16 Top, Lam Tom, Cover Back, leocalvett, Cover, 1,
(Globe), ludmilafoto, 1 TR, Mikadun, 1 TL, 10, Monkey Business Images,
15, 20 Top, Nagy-Bagoly Arpad, 12 Bottom, NigelSpiers, 8 Bottom,
Ninelle, 28, Nolte Lourens, Cover TR, 3 BL, OlegD, 9 BL, Pablo Rogat, 5,
Paolo Bona, 6 BR, R.M. Nunes, Cover BL, racorn, 14 TR, Rafal Cichawa,
9 Right, Robyn Butler, 20 Bottom, Sergey Novikov, 21, Sokolova Maryna,
8 Top, Stawek, 30, sunsinger, 24 TR, Vladimir Wrangel, 24 Bottom,
withGod, 7, 25, XiXinXing, 29, Zzvet, 3 TR; SuperStock: age fotostock,
27 Bottom, Charles O. Cecil/age fotostock, 3 TL, Robert Harding Picture
Library, 9 TL, Travel Pix Collection/Jon Arnold Images, 16 Bottom,
Walter Zerla/age fotostock, 22 Bottom.

READ MORE

**Ajmera, Maya, Elise Hofer Derstine, and
Cynthia Pon.** *What We Wear: Dressing
Up Around the World.* Watertown,
Mass.: Charlesbridge, 2012.

Lewis, Clare. *Clothes Around the World.*
Around the World. Chicago: Heinemann
Library, 2015.

Spilsbury, Louise. *World Cultures.*
Investigate. Chicago: Heinemann
Library, 2010.

INTERNET SITES

FactHound offers a safe, fun way to
find Internet sites related to this book.
All of the sites on FactHound have been
researched by our staff.

Here's all you do:
Visit *www.facthound.com*
Type in this code:
9781491439173

Check out projects, games and lots more at
www.capstonekids.com

Printed in China.
032015   008864WMF15